BERLIN
AND POTSDAM

Photographs: Schikkus Archive and Siebrand Reheberg Fotodesign.

Text, layout and reproduction:
EDITORIAL FISA ESCUDO DE ORO, S.A.

Photograph, text and translation copyright of this edition:
© SCHIKKUS Verlag & Großhandel GmbH & Co. KG
© EDITORIAL FISA ESCUDO DE ORO, S.A.

SCHIKKUS
VERLAG & GROSSHANDEL GmbH & Co. KG
Tel: (030) 364 077-0 - Fax: 3640 77 77
www.schikkus.de

ESCUDO DE ORO

2

BERLIN

With close to 3.4 million inhabitants and a surface area of 890 km², Berlin is both the biggest city in Germany and the city with the highest population density. 40% of the city is made up of parks, woods and garden areas which, together with the Spree and Havel rivers and an intricate canal network, paint a beautiful urban landscape in the middle of a green and blue oasis.

Berlin's history dates back to 1237, the year when the existence of two merchant towns by the banks of the Spree River, Cölln and Berlin, was first documented. In 1307, both towns became united politically, beginning a stage of great economic development. The new city became known as Berlin. Although it is not entirely certain where the name originates from, some sources link it with the word *Bär*, German for 'bear', and others with the mixture of Slavonic terms *Bar* (woods) and *rolina* (crop field). A member of the Hanseatic League since the second half of the 14th century, the

Aerial view of Oberbaum Bridge and the Television Tower.

city was chosen by the Hohenzollern dynasty for their place of residence, and they would remain there until the fall of the monarchy in 1918.

Berlin's growth was brought to an abrupt halt by the Thirty Years' War (1618-1648), when 6,000 Berliners, almost half of the population, lost their lives. However, the city began to recover from this tragedy in the next few years, through the encouragement provided by Prince Friedrich Wilhelm "The Great Elector". He opened the city doors to the people of Europe, and in particular to the French Huguenots, Viennese Jews, the Dutch, Bohemians and the Flemish. His son, Friedrich, proclaimed himself the first King of Prussia in 1701, giving Berlin the status of a royal residence. Both this monarch and his successor, Friedrich II, commissioned great architectural works in order to place the city on a par with the other European capitals. The expression "Athens on the Spree", often used to refer to Berlin, originated during this period because of the predominant style used for building these works.

The 19th century was one of extraordinary prosperity, the era in which the industrial and cul-

Brandenburg Gate and the Sony Center (Potsdam Square).

Berlin has an extensive transport network. The S-Bahn and the U-Bahn are shown in the photographs.

tural bases of 20th century Berlin took root. The defeat in the First World War put an end to the monarchy in Germany, and meant exile for Friedrich II, the last Kaiser of the Hohenzollern dynasty. In 1920, the Greater Berlin Act was passed and 8 cities, 59 communities and 27 rural districts were incorporated into the old city on that date. During these years, the city's population reached 3.9 million. As the capital of the Third Reich, Berlin suffered the devastating effects of the Second World War. When Germany surrendered on 2nd May 1945, the once-proud city had become the largest ruin in Europe. Divided in four sections by the victors, the outbreak of another conflict, the Cold War, led the communist authorities of the German Democratic Republic (GDR) to make the drastic decision of erecting a wall which separated the part under its control from the rest of the city. This occurred on the sad night of 13 August 1961, a long night that would last until 9 November 1989, the day the Wall ceased to make sense and stopped dividing the Berliners. On 3rd October 1990, Germany became a single state once more and in 1999, Berlin was made the official capital.

Another appealing way of visiting the city is in one of the boats that travel down the Spree.

THE BERLIN WALL

On the night of 13 August 1961, the authorities of the GDR decided to close off the part of the city under its control with barbed wire fences. That same night, the construction of a concrete wall began. A wall 165 kilometres long and 3.5 metres high that would mark the life of all its residents for 28 long years. Families separated, friendships torn apart and a deep feeling of infinite sadness alternating with indignation that scorched the mind and soul of the Berliners and all other Germans, were just some of the consequences of this open wound in the heart of

9

Images of the Wall before its demolition.

YOU ARE LEAVING
THE AMERICAN SECTOR
ВЫ ВЫЕЗЖАЕТЕ ИЗ
АМЕРИКАНСКОГО СЕКТОРА
VOUS SORTEZ
DU SECTEUR AMÉRICAIN
SIE VERLASSEN DEN AMERIKANISCHEN SEKTOR
US ARMY

the German capital. The most tragic consequence, however, was the death of 255 people who lost their lives trying to cross the wall. This irrational nightmare, this cruel example of human stupidity, officially ended at 11.15 pm on 9 November 1989 when the gates of the wall were opened, and an air of freedom and reconciliation passed through them.

Fortunately, the Berlin Wall is now history. Although it was almost completely dismantled in the months after it fell, there are still fragments of it in different parts of the city today. The largest part is found in Mühlenstraße Street, to the north of the centre. In other areas, marks on the ground from paint or red ceramics are reminders of where the wall once stood.

Next to the famous **Checkpoint Charlie** border crossing in Friedrichstraße, which has been preserved as a reminder, the **Wall Museum** presents some of the methods of crossing the barrier devised by the citizens of the East and abundant documentation on everything concerning its construction and the sad years of the division. The **Oberbaumbrücke** (Oberbaum Bridge) was another famous east-west control point and exchange place for spies and political prisoners during the Cold War. It was reconstructed following the Second World War after being blown up by Hitler's Wehrmacht. The full restoration of the bridge was finished in 1994.

UNTER DEN LINDEN

The elegant Unter den Linden boulevard is one of the main hubs in the area known as *Berlin Mitte* situated right in the middle (hence its name) of the historic centre of what is now the great German capital. Almost one and a half kilometres long and sixty metres wide, the name of this emblematic avenue in Berlin, "under the lime trees", refers to the lime and walnut trees that were planted in 1647 to line the road that joined the Royal Palace to Tiergarten.

Brandenburg Gate was built between 1788 and 1791 by architect Carl Gotthard Langhans (who took his inspiration from the Acropolis in Athens) at the request of King Friedrich Wilhelm II, who wanted to pay homage to Frederick the Great, the monarch of peace, through the work. The gate was crowned with a bronze sculpture of a chariot drawn by four horses, and driven by the goddess of Victory. In 1807, Napoleon took this piece as war loot and it was not returned to its original place until 1814, the year the Prussian army defeated the French in the

Brandenburg Gate and the United States Embassy.

battle of Leipzig. The iron cross and the eagle figure were added then.

The **Paris Square** dates from this same year, even if the majority of the buildings surrounding it nowadays are contemporary: the **Academy of Arts**, a large glass building which opened to the public in 2005, the **DG Bank** headquarters (1997-99) designed by Frank Gehry, the **French Embassy** (1999-2001), by Christian de Portzampac, and the **British Embassy** (1997-2000), by Michael Wilford. The **Hotel Adlon**, inaugurated in 1904, also stands out, although it was completely rebuilt in 1997, preserving the original design of the façades. The first buildings in Unter der Linden are the **embassies** of some eastern European countries. The most magnificent is the Russian embassy, erected in 1953 when Stalin's Soviet Union was at its peak.

Further along Unter den Linden is **Humboldt University**, originally the palace where Frederick the Great's brother Prince Heinrich lived. It was built between 1748 and 1766, and was converted into a university when the prince died in 1809. It is named after its founder, German politician and philologist Wilhelm von Humboldt. Across from the university on the other pave-

The horse-drawn chariot on Brandenburg Gate.

The old Royal Library.

ment of Unter den Linden is the **Bebelplatz**. This square is the centre of the Frederick Forum, an urban development conceived by Frederick the Great where the buildings would serve as a testimony to the cultural growth of 18th century Prussia. Originally, the forum included the **Hedwigskathedrale** (Catholic Cathedral of Saint Hedvig, a building inspired by the Roman Pantheon), the **Staatsoper** (State Opera) and the **Könichliche Bibliothek** (Royal Library, built in the image and likeness of the Imperial Palace in Vienna, now a law faculty), but it has grown larger as time passed and now encompasses more buildings. The **equestrian statue of Frederick the Great** dominates the square, a monument dating from 1851 also featuring such personalities from the era as Prince Leopold I, the philosopher Kant and

17

Equestrian statue of Frederick the Great.

writer Gotthold Ephraim Lessing. The **Sunken Library**, created by Micha Ullmann in 1995, is another monument which reminds us that the square was the setting for the infamous book burning ordered by Goebbels on 10 May 1933. It consists of an empty library, built into the ground, symbolising the intellectual vacuum produced by National Socialism in Germany with the persecution of writers and intellectuals.

Continuing along Unter den Linden after Humboldt University, is the **Neue Wache** (New Guard House), a station that Friedrich Wilhelm ordered be built in 1816. Today, it is the site of a monument erected in memory of the victims of the Nazis and militarism. The sculpture, created by Käthe Kollwith, was inspired by Michaelangelo's *Pieta*.

Next to this old military installation is the **Zeughaus** (Arsenal), an early 18th century building which is one of main gems of the Baroque period in the entire country. The **German History Museum** has existed since the time of the GDR.

We now arrive at the **Schlossbrücke** (Palace Bridge), a work dating from 1824 designed by great German architect Karl Friedrich Schinkel, who was also responsible for the eight marble

19

The Palace Bridge with the old Arsenal, today the German History Museum, in the background.

sculptures that adorn it. For those interested in Schinkel, whose architecture is considered the main reason behind Berlin's nickname "the Athens of the Spree", a nearby museum displays his impressive work as a sculptor. The building, designed by Schinkel himself, is an old church restored in 1980.

After the bridge, Unter den Linden reaches Karl-Liebknecht Avenue. The **Royal Palace** was situated here, but it was very badly damaged during the Second World War, and completely demolished by the GDR authorities in 1950. The Palace of the Republic, the site of the GDR Parliament, was built in its place in 1970. However, this building suffered the same fate and was demolished in 2006. There is currently an ambitious project underway to rebuild the former Hohenzollern palace. On the other side of the street, and continuing on from the cathedral, is the **Dom Aquaree**, a block-long building completed in 2004 that includes a hotel, offices, a commercial gallery and housing. The highlight of this complex is found in the hotel patio. the AquaDom, a gigantic clear glass cylinder 25 metres high and 11.5 metres wide, where countless tropical fish swim in a million litres of salt water.

21

GENDARMENMARKT

This square is considered the most beautiful in Berlin. Gendarmenmarkt shines both for the beauty of its monuments as well as its magnificent surroundings. The Gens d'Armes Cuirassiers (mounted cavalry) regiment had their headquarters and stables here between 1736 and 1782, and gave the square its name. Some years before, Friedrich Wilhelm I had ordered the building of the two cathedrals that still dominate the square today. In 1785, identical domes were added to them. The Huguenots, who were exiled from France by Louis XIV, designed the **Französische Dom** (French Cathedral). The Huguenots Museum was added when it was being restored in 1984. The **Deutsche Dom** (German Cathedral) also hosts a permanent exhibition focusing on some excerpts from the country's history dating from 1800. Friedrich Wilhelm II had the **Konzerthaus** erected between the two houses of worship in 1774. In 1817, Schinkel's masterpiece went up in flames and the Second World War left it in ruins. The current building is a reconstruction from 1967.

Gendarmenmarkt: the German Cathedral and the Konzerthaus.

FRIEDRICHSTRAßE

During the first few decades of the twentieth century, a good deal of the business world, political activity and the leisure options available in the city were concentrated along the Friedrichstraße. The bombings during the Second World War and the later construction of the Wall left the street semi-abandoned, a state it only began to emerge from in the early 1990s with the rehabilitation of many buildings and the construction of new ones. Modern iron and glass buildings housing the never-ending commercial centres, dominate the area around Unter der Linden, the most famous ones being the **Galeries Lafayette.** Further up the street is **Friedrichstraße Station,** one of the most frequently used border crossing points during the years Berlin was divided. The customs control was done in a nearby building called Tränenpalast (Palace of Tears) because of the countless sad farewells that took place there. Now that painful era is well and truly in the past, and it has been transformed into a lively commercial and cultural centre.

Inside the Quartier 206 galleries. On the left, a tower built of crushed auto bodies, a piece by John Chamberlain.

ISLAND OF MUSEUMS

The **Lustgarten** gardens, formerly the Royal Palace gardens, are the prelude to the Museumsinsel (Island of Museums). This relatively small island (almost 1 km^2) is mostly surrounded by the Spree and contains five of the best museums in Berlin. The **Berliner Dom** (Berlin Cathedral) is also found here. One of Wilhelm II's initiatives, the church was built between 1894 and 1905 by architects Julius Carl and Otto Raschdorff, who used Saint Peter's Basîlica in Rome as a reference to erect what had to be the most important Protestant church in Germany, and also the mausoleum for the Hohenzollern dynasty. The presence of several styles, with Renaissance art and Baroque predominant, the four corner towers and the large central dome are its main charms.

The **Alte Museum** (Old Museum) was built between 1824 and 1830 by Schinkel, who carried out a magnificent recreation of the Greek buildings from the classical period. Its beautiful rotunda and ionic columns are an excellent introduction to the magnificent collections of sculptures and paintings it displays. A few

The Bode Museum from the Spree.

years later, the **Neue Museum** (New Museum) opened its doors. This museum also offers interesting examples of ancient art. The **Alte Nationalgalerie** (Old National Gallery) dates from 1876 and is a beautiful neoclassical construction presided over by the equestrian statue of Friedrich Wilhelm.

The **Pergamonmuseum** (Pergamon Museum) is one of the most important archaeology museums in the world. It was built between 1912 and 1930 to hold the fascinating Pergamon Altar, which belonged to a temple in this Greek city, now in Turkish territory, discovered by a German archaeological expedition at the end of the 19th century. Other highlights of the museum include the Market Gate of Miletus, the Ishtar Gate which provided access to the legendary city of Babylon, and the decorative panelling from a Syrian palace.

Lastly, the **Bodemuseum** (Bode Museum) was opened in 1904 and displays very interesting collections of papyrus, coins, paintings and sculptures. The museum is named after art historian and museologist Wilhem von Bode, who was responsible for the project of the building and its contents.

29

Equestrian statue of Friedrich Wilhelm IV.

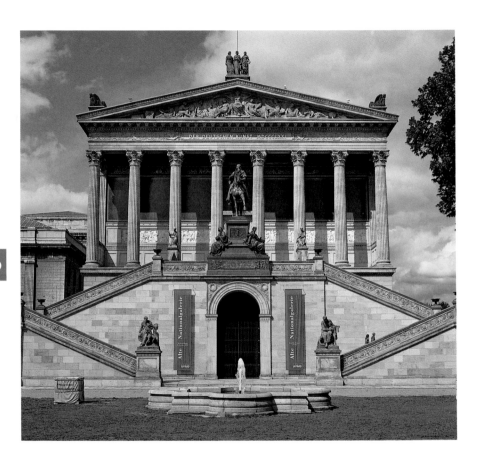

Old National Gallery.

Pergamon Museum: Babylon Gate, Pergamon Altar and overview of the building.

Saint Nicholas District: Overview, Church of Saint Nicholas, sculpture of the Berlin bear and a typical street.

SAINT NICHOLAS DISTRICT

After the Marx-Engels Forum and next to the Spree, is the small, peaceful Saint Nicholas district with its typical houses, terraces and antique shops. This is where Cölln, one of the towns which merged to form Berlin, once stood. Destroyed during the Second World War, the GDR authorities decided to rebuild it in 1987 to coincide with the 750th anniversary of the founding of the city. The **Church of Saint Nicholas** dating from 1230 dominates the area. Opposite the church is the famous **sculpture of the Berlin bear** holding the city shield in his paws. Also in this area is the **Zum Nussbaum** (Walnut) inn, moved from another part of the city in 1571, and the **Ephraim-Palais,** a rococo palace from 1764 owned by the wealthy and controversial Veitel-Heine Ephraim. For years, this powerful character enjoyed the right to the title of Mint Master of Berlin. However, his ambition grew out of control and led to his downfall when he replaced the gold used to cover the coins with a thin golden layer.

Sculpture of Saint George and the Dragon.

MARX-ENGELS-FORUM AND ALEXANDERPLATZ

The **Marx-Engels-Forum** is a spacious square, dominated by the statues of the two fathers of socialism since 1986. In one of the corners is the unmistakeable façade of the **Rote Rathaus** (Red Town Hall), named for the colour of the bricks used to build it between 1861 and 1869. It has a magnificent tower 97 metres high, and a terracotta frieze, visible from outside, evoking the history of the city since its foundation until 1871, the year the Reich was formed. In front of the building is the **Fountain of Neptune**, a sculpture with references to what were the four most important rivers in Prussia at the end of the 19th century: Rhine, Elbe, Oder and Vistula. On the other side of the square is the **Marienkirche** (Church of Saint Mary), a 13th century church which has undergone many renovations over the years. During one of these reforms, a painting from the 15th century which includes different scenes relat-

Marx-Engels-Forum: The Television Tower and the Red Town Hall tower are "observed" by Marx and Engels.

Alexanderplatz: World Clock.

ed to dance and death was found The Neo-gothic tower rising from the building dates from 1790.

However, the building that stands out most in the square is the **Fernsehturm** (Television Tower). It is 365 metres high and visible from any point in the city. It was inaugurated in 1969 and has a rotating viewpoint 200 metres above the ground. The views looking over all of Berlin are spectacular.

The adjoining **Alexanderplatz** is also very large. Its name commemorates Tsar Alexander I of Russia's visit to Berlin in 1805. During the division, the city became the centre of East Berlin, although it turned into a slightly cold and impersonal place. To counter that, the **Weltzeituhr** (World Clock), which gives the time in 27 different locations in the world, and the **Fountain of Friendship between Peoples** were both added in 1967.

37

Fernsehturm (Television Tower).

Hackesche Höfe: Façade of Oranienburger Straße.

Sculpture opposite the Town Theatre, in Rosa-Luxemburg-Platz.

HACKESCHER MARKT AND ORANIENBURGER STREET

Together with the nearby Alexanderplatz, **Hackescher Markt** is a main meeting point in Berlin Mitte, since it has both an underground and train station. The building that now shelters the station was once a market, erected in 1906 by General von Hacke, hence the name. Hackesche Markt today is also a square surrounded by cafés, restaurants and businesses, teeming with human activity, day and night. In nearby Oranienburger Street are the famous **Hackesche Höfe**. These are the inside patios of the residences connected to one another that were built, like many others at the end of the 19th century, to accommodate the new arrivals to the city who sought one of the numerous job vacancies being generated by an industrial sector in full growth. The houses belonging to these patios (*höfe*), known as "renting quarters" (*mietskasernen*), were generally very humble, although the Hackesche quarters were an exception.

39

Hackescher Markt terraces, traditional meeting point among Berliners.

The **Oranienburger Straße** gives us an idea of the vitality of the alternative cultural movements taking place in Berlin. After the fall of the Wall, a group of squatter founded the **Kunsthaus Tacheles** cultural centre in this street, with the aim of offering new possibilities to those who had a groundbreaking vision of art.

Another place worth noting in Oranienburgerstraße is the **New Synagogue**. What was once a magnificent and luxurious building built in 1866, and a social and spiritual centre for Berlin Jews from that point on, miraculously survived the tragic Kristallnacht (Night of Broken Glass) on 9 November 1938. However, the bombings during the Second World War left only the façade standing. Work began to restore the synagogue in 1988 and, seven years later, its doors were opened once again as the Centrum Judaicum (Jewish Centre). The present site is not only a synagogue but also has a museum dedicated to the life of Jews in Berlin.

Between Oranienburgerstraße and the river Spree is the beautiful **Monbijou Park**, which boasts the **Strandbad-Mitte**, a very crowded city beach on sunny days.

Domes of the New Synagogue.
The Strandbad–Mitte, next to the Spree.

TIERGARTEN

With a surface area of 235 hectares, Tiergarten is the oldest park in Berlin and also its great "green lung". Once the private hunting ground for the Electors of Brandenburg, Tiergarten was opened to the public in 1717 by Friedrich I, the first king of Prussia. At the beginning of the 19th century, it experienced a total and ambitious restructuring at the hands of the great landscape architect Peter Joseph Lenné, who used the classic English garden as a model. Destroyed during the Second World War and with most of the trees felled for firewood for those cold postwar winters, a reconstruction faithful to Lenné's original idea began in 1949. Paths, canals, hundreds of thousands of trees and the Neuer See, a large lake where one can take a boat trip, make up this delightful oasis that is much loved and visited by Berliners. **17 June Avenue**, a name recalling the date of a revolt by workers in East Berlin in 1953, divides Tiergarten in two. Monuments and some of the headquarters of political institutions are found in the north-

Aerial view of Tiergarten.

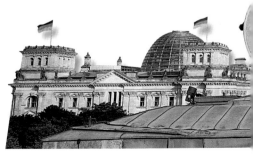

The Reichstag, detail of the dome, work of Norman Foster (1994–1999), and view of the horse-drawn chariot on Brandenburg Gate.

ern part, while the park's greatest natural attractions are in the south. On Saturdays and Sundays, the **Kunst- und Trödelmarkt** (an art object and used items market) takes place in this avenue. It is the largest street market in the German capital.

The **Reichstag** is at the eastern edge Tiergarten, to the north of Brandenburg Gate. It was built between 1884 and 1894 by architect Paul Wallot to give the Prussian Empire formed in 1871 a home for its House of Representatives. This majestic Parliament has borne witness to many of the historical events that the country endured in the last century. For example, the Republic was proclaimed from one of its balconies in 1918. Fifteen years later, it was partially damaged by a fire that the Nazi regime blamed on the Communists. In 1945, the Soviet troops marked the fall of Hitler's Germany by raising the red flag there. Finally, welcomed the first parliamentary meeting after the reunification of the two Germanys in 1990.

The Reichstag later underwent an extensive restora-

tion project directed by English architect Norman Foster. He is the man behind the spectacular 23-metre-high glass dome that replaced the original one and is visited by thousands of tourists on a daily basis. An original system employing mirrors allows natural light to enter and fully illuminate the room.

The **Soviet Monument** is also located in 17 June Avenue near the Reichstag. It was unveiled shortly after the war to pay homage to the nearly 20,000 soldiers from the Red Army who died in the conquest of Berlin. This solemn building was in an Allied area during the division of the city, creating great tension during the bitter years of the Cold War.

The **Holocaust-Mahnmal** (Memorial to the Murdered Jews of Europe) was opened in May 2005 next to the Eberstraße, where the Wall once passed. This structure created by American architect Peter Eisenmann is composed of 2,711 concrete blocks of different

The Federal Chancellery from the Spree.

Detail on the Soviet Monument.

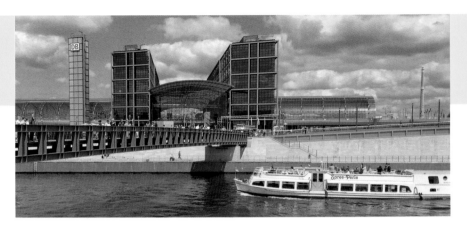

Berlin Central Station.

Holocaust Memorial, the
Reichstag and Berlin
Central Station.

sizes organised in rows like a graveyard. There is also an information centre where the persecution of the Jews by the Nazi regime is documented.

There are several government buildings in the northern part of Tiergarten. The **Bundeskanzleramt** (Federal Chancellery), designed by architect Axel Schultes and unveiled in 2001, stands out for its postmodern cubic form. The **Berlin Hauptbahnhof-Lehrter Bahnhof** (Berlin Central Station), opened in May 2006 and the largest connecting railway station in Europe, is also situated in the north of Tiergarten. The complex, designed by architect Meinhard von Gerkan, has a total surface area of 70,000 m², spread among five floors of 15,000 m². Every day, some 500 trains pass through the north-south axis, 250 go along the east-west route, as well as 1,000 trams and underground trains. The **Haus der Kulturen der Welt** (House of World Cultures), christened by Berliners as "the pregnant oyster" for its unusual design, is also worth noting. It originally was the United States contribution to the International Building Exhi-

House of World Cultures.

Tiergarten: Bellevue Palace and the Otto von Bismarck monument, work of Reinhold Begas in 1901.

bition (Interbau) in 1957. It is a venue for exhibitions, concerts and conferences.

Towards the west, **Bellevue Palace** rises from a landscape of trees and gardens. It has been the official residence of the German President since 1993. This neoclassical-style building built in 1786 had a famous tenant; Ferdinand of Prussia, Frederick the Great's younger brother.

Five important avenues in Berlin converge in the middle of Tiergarten. The **Siegessäule** (Victory Column), built in 1873, rises from this crossroad known as the **Großer Stern** (Big Star). Some 70 metres high, the column is crowned with a golden figure of the goddess Victoria weighing around 35 tonnes. A spiral staircase leads up to the statue's feet, where there is a viewpoint. The monument, erected to commemorate the success of the Prussian army, was originally situated in Republic Square. In 1938, Hitler ordered the column to be moved.

51

The Victory Column: the Goddess of Victory.

KULTURFORUM

The division of the city in two halves left West Berlin without the great cultural reference of the nucleus formed by the Island of Museums and Unter den Linden Avenue. To fill that void, a plan began to take shape in the early ´60s to erect a series of buildings in the southern part of Tiergarten to house different cultural institutions. Architect Hans Scharoun (1893-1972) was in charge of the overall project. He had already worked on the reconstruction of the German capital in 1946. The first building finished was the **Berliner Philharmonie** (concert hall), the home venue for the legendary Berlin Philharmonic Orchestra since it opened in 1963. The **Kammermusiksaal** (Chamber Music Hall), built in 1987 following plans designed by Scharoun, and the **Instrument Museum** dating from were built next to the concert house. Opposite them is the **Museum of Applied Arts** in a building built between 1973 and 1985 by architect Rolf Gutbrod. The **Engravings Hall** and the **Painting Gallery** were added to the

Overview of the Kulturforum: on the left, the Philharmonic Hall and on the right, the Church of Saint Matthias.

complex in 1994 and 1998, respectively. The former building recounts the evolution of graphic arts from the Middle Ages to the present, and the Painting Gallery includes one of the most complete retrospectives of European painting in its 56 rooms.

Between 1965 and 1968, the glass and steel pavilion of Mies van der Rohe's **New National Gallery** was erected next to the **Church of Saint Matthias**, which dates from 1846 and is used today as an exhibition hall. This installation displays both the permanent collections of the most representative examples of German surrealism and expressionism, and other temporary collections that share an extraordinary quality.

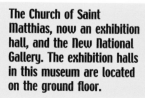

The Church of Saint Matthias, now an exhibition hall, and the New National Gallery. The exhibition halls in this museum are located on the ground floor.

POTSDAM SQUARE

Located on the other side of the Cultural Forum, **Potsdam Square** was an immense site almost completely lacking in buildings during the years of the Wall. It was little more than a vague memory in the minds who saw its customary hustle and bustle before the war, full of vehicles and pedestrians, as well as the underground, trains, and 26 tram lines which used to pass through there. In 1994, this space began to fill up with lorries, cranes and preparations for future projects. In order to carry out the radical transformation, renowned architects such as Arata Isozaki, Renzo Piano, Helmut Jahn, Hans Kollhoff, Rafael Moneo and Santiago Calatrava were called upon. Multinational companies such as Daimler Chrysler, ABB and Sony bought hectares of land to build offices, business centres and other services. Six years later, the square had taken on a completely different look, full of flats hotels, cinemas, theatres, shops, restaurants, cafés, a casino and large office blocks. The **Sony Cen-**

Overview of Potsdam Square: On the right, the Sony Center, in the centre, the Deutsche Bahn (DB) building, with Daimler-Chrysler City in the background.

ter is one of the highlights with its large indoor patio, sheltered by a roof that changes colour. It contains the latest audiovisual technology, as well as the cinema programmes of the German Filmotec (film library) based there and the IMAX cinemas.

Anhalter Station, in nearby Askanischer square, is a reminder of the energy and dynamism that once existed in this part of the city. Up until the war, it was Berlin's main railway station and the third largest in Europe. Anhalter Bahnhof was very badly damaged during the war and closed definitively in 1952. The remains of the main façade have been preserved and the **Tempodrom**, an auditorium in the shape of a circus tent, was opened in 2001 where the tracks used to be.

BREITSCHEIDPLATZ AND KU'DAMM

Breitscheidplatz is a noisy square which became the nerve centre of "West-Berlin". The city's main commercial avenues, the famous Ku'damm and Tauentzienstraße, converge here, resulting in a constant presence of street artists. The square is dominated by the **Kaiser-Wilhelm-Gedächt-niskirche** (Kaiser Wilhelm Memorial Church). This Neo-Romanesque temple is both the symbol of the past glory of one era, and the modern drive of another. It was built between 1891 and 1895 in honour of the Kaiser Wilhelm I and is popu-larly known as "the hollow tooth". It was badly damaged by the bombings during the war and architect Egon Eiermann was commissioned to restore it in 1957. Although it was a controver-sial decision, he left the ruined tower standing and erected another hexagonal one, plus a new church with an octagonal foundation. The buildings, created between 1961 and 1963 using steel and blue glass, were soon christened "the lipstick and powder puff" by Berliners.

Aerial view of the centre of "West-Berlin".

Breitscheidplatz: the "Terrestrial Globe", 18 m in diameter and 4.5 m high, dates from 1983.

Europa–Center: The Clock of Flowing Time.

The **Europa-Center** is situated at the junction with Tauenzienstraße and dates from 1965. With more than one hundred shops, numerous restaurants and cafés, hotels and offices, this "city within a city" was the first skyscraper built in West Berlin after the war. The Mercedes-Benz company logo crowns the 103 metre high building. Two of the main attractions are the Cafe Tiffany's terrace and the "Clock of Flowing Time". Three very famous department stores are found in Tauenzienstraße: **Tauentzienpalast** (1931), **Peek & Cloppenburg** (1995) and especially Kaufhaus des Westens, better known as **KaDeWe** (1906). After the reforms were carried out at the end of the Second World War, the KaDeWe became one of the largest commercial areas in all of Europe. The sixth floor, suggestively named "gourmet paradise", still has a legendary reputation.

63

On the other side of the Breitscheidplatz, occupying a large part of the southwest end of Tiergarten, is the **Zoological Garden** housing over 1,500 animal species. It was designed in 1840 by P.J. Lenné, the same landscape artist who created Tiergarten. Highlights include the

Tauenzienstraße: The Berlin sculpture is a composition integrated by the broken links of a chain that was installed here in 1987 to mark the city's 750th anniversary.

Interior patio of the Victoria Passage and the Zoo Aquarium.

Elephant Gate.

Elephant Gate and the charming Aquarium building.

Kurfürstendamm, commonly referred to as Ku'damm, is the commercial avenue "par excellence" in Berlin. This four-kilometre-long avenue contains not only the most select and exclusive shops and boutiques, but also the best prices. Until 1880, Ku'damm was simply a dirt street that connected the city with the Electors' hunting palace. Otto von Bismarck ordered it to be developed, so that the German capital would have a great avenue just like the other European capitals. The **Wertheim** department stores, with their panoramic restaurant, are among the most famous locations in this street. The **Café Kranzler** also enjoys a view of the daily activity in Ku'damm due to its privileged position on the corner with Joachimstalerstraße.

The Ku'damm-Karree galleries, located by the Adenauerplatz, display **"The Story of Berlin"** exhibition. An impeccable presentation and the use of advanced technology allow visitors to be submerged in the landscapes that have marked Berlin's history.

The Kranzler Café and the DIFA building, work of Helmut Jahn in 2006.

CHARLOTTENBURG

This area was still a residential district of Berlin in the middle of the countryside when Prince-Elector Friedrich, later Friedrich I of Prussia, decided to build a summer palace here for his wife Sophie-Charlotte at the end of the 17th century. Work on the palace by architect Johann Arnold Nering began in 1695. However, starting from 1701 and coinciding with Friedrich of Prussia's rise to the throne, the building was renovated and enlarged on various occasions throughout the 18th century. The palace was named **Schloss Charlottenburg** by Friedrich in 1705, in memory of his wife who died that year when she was just 36 years old. The area surrounding the palace, from Tiergarten to the Olympic Stadium, would also come to be known by that name. However, like the rest of the city, what was one of the most brilliant examples of Baroque art in Berlin was reduced almost to ruins during the Second World War. After the authorities in East-Berlin demolished the remaining part of the Royal Palace in the city centre in 1950, it was decided to carry out

Charlottenburg Palace.

Charlottenburg Palace: detail of the entrance railing, the Belvedere Tea House, statue of Friedrich II and aerial view.

a faithful reconstruction following the original plans in order to restore it to its former splendour. That is how the sole surviving Hohenzollern site preserved in the German capital was saved. The palace fascinates visitors today because of its sumptuous rooms and exquisite park, created by P.J. Lenné in a modern English style.

During the 19th century, several barracks were built opposite the palace that are now the sites of different museums: the **Egyptian Museum** (its most famous pieces are the busts of Nefertiti, her husband Akhenaten, and Queen Tiye), the **Berggruen Museum** (with paintings by Cézanne, Van Gogh, Picasso, Klee, Matisse and Giacometti, among others) and the **Bröhan Museum** (featuring the extensive collection of paintings, sculptures, furniture and porcelain from the period between 1889 and 1940 obtained by businessman Kart Bröhan).

Next to the Messedamm are the different pavilions of the exhibition centre and the avantgarde **International Conference Centre (ICC)** building. It was built in 1975 and has extraordinary dimensions: 320 metres long, 80 metres wide and 40 metres high. In the middle of this complex stands the "lanky lad" (Langen Lulatsch),

The Communications Tower next to the International Conference Centre (ICC).

Concert in the Theatre in the Woods (Waldbühne).

Mayfield Belltower, next to the Olympic Stadium, viewpoint 77.17 m above the ground.

as Berliners call the **Communications Tower**. It was unveiled in 1926 at the 3rd Great German Radio Exhibition. Its full height, including the antenna, reaches 150 metres. It boasts a restaurant at 55 metres, and a viewpoint near the top.

In 1912, the **Olympic Stadium** where the athletics events of the 1916 Olympic Games were going to be held was built to the west of Charlottenburg. Unfortunately, the event never took place because of the outbreak of the First World War. Twenty years later, Berlin was elected again to host this sports event. Architects Werner and Walter March, the sons of Otto March, who designed the original stadium, took charge of the renovation. The capacity was increased from 47,000 spectators to 100,000, and the stadium itself was expanded to 300 metres long and 230 metres wide.

Different cultural events were taking place at the same time as the 1936 Olympic Games. Operas were being held in the **Waldbühne** (Theatre in the Woods), an open-air amphitheatre in the ancient Greek style with a capacity of 20,000 people built behind the stadium. Today, Waldbühne is one of the favourite meeting places for Berliners and is also a site for rock festivals.

The Olympic Stadium was completely restored in 2006 for the Football World Cup.

WOODS AND LAKES IN BERLIN

There is a large area of woods and lakes west of the city, accessible from the centre in just a few minutes via the S-Bahn, and particularly popular with Berliners on Sundays and holidays. **Grunewald** (green wood) makes up the great "green lung" in this part of Berlin, occupying an area of 32 km² between the built-up area of the city and the Havel River. A motorway built in 1909 passes through it. There are two excellent viewpoints overlooking Grunewald and the Havel in the western half: the **Grunewaldturm**, a neo-Gothic brick tower standing 50 metres high and the **Teufelsberg**, a 120-metre-high artificial hill made with 25 million cubic metres of rubble and debris removed from bombed-out Berlin after the war.

South of Grunewald, the Havel expands to form a bay called **Großer Wannsee**, ideal for swimming and hiring boats. In summer, the long sandy **beach** of Wannsee, a large island south of the bay, is filled with Berliners who come to spend

Grunewald Tower: 204 steps lead up to the 40 metres high viewpoint.

Pfaueninsel Castle, in Peacock Island.

Glienicke Palace, designed by Schinkel.

the day there. Others opt for boats trips along the Havel: either north to Spandau and Tegel or south to Pfaueninsel, Glienicke and Potsdam. The **Pfaueninsel** (Peacock Island), 1.5 kilometres long and 500 metres wide, is a very beautiful natural reserve, dotted with paths, gardens, small palaces and a charming castle which Friedrich Wilhelm III built for his lover, Countess Lichtenau, in 1797. Lenné, the same landscape artist who created Tiergarten and the Charlottenburg gardens, designed the idyllic, English-style park surrounding the castle. The island's name comes from the colony of peacocks living there.

Glienicke Bridge was built during the rule of Friedrich Wilhelm and is 300 metres long. It was blown up during the last few days of the war by German troops and rebuilt in 1950. The bridge was the setting for frequent exchanges of secret agents in the following years. The nearby **Glienicke Palace**, a neoclassical building dating from 1824, was a gift from Queen Louise to her son Charles. The English garden surrounding it was another Lenné creation.

The old town of **Spandau** was incorporated into the city of Berlin in 1920, even though its

Glienicke Bridge.

Partial aerial view of Spandau, by the banks of the Sharfe Lanke bay.

250,000 inhabitants still maintain their pride as residents of a district whose origins as a town date to 1232. The old historic centre (Altstadt) preserves beautiful examples of its medieval past such as the 15th century **Church of Saint Nicholas** and the 16th century **Citadel**.

The other great green area of the city is located to the southeast, in the **Köpenick** district. You could say that Berlin assumes the role of a somewhat peaceful village here, due to the presence of houses with large gardens, vividly green woods, small islands, two rivers (the Spree and the Dahme) and the 7.5 km^2 Großer Müggelsee, the largest lake in the city.

The Spree is a river that Berliners like to enjoy by either travelling down it in a boat or sunbathing on its banks. Some swimming pools have even been built at different points along the river. Next to the Elsen Bridge, the **Molecule Man** sculpture, a piece by American artist Jonathan Borofsky from 1999, emerges from the water. It is made of aluminium and stands 30 metres high. The three human figures symbolise the point where the three districts of Treptow, Friedrichshain and Kreuzberg meet.

"Molecule Man" sculpture.

THEATRES AND MUSEUMS IN BERLIN

The vast cultural offer available is one of Berlin's main attractions. This includes a wide ranging programme of festivals in addition to 3 opera theatres, over 150 theatres and stages, some 800 choirs, over 175 museums and collections, 300 private galleries, 250 public libraries, and around 150 cinema halls. Every year around six million people visit Berlin's museums and about three million attend its theatre productions.

The **Theater des Westens** (Theatre of the west) in Kantstraße, which started up in 1896, is particularly noteworthy. During its first few years, this splendid Belle Epoque building housed operatic performances and later became a hotspot for famous musicals. Friedrichstraße and the neighbouring surrounding streets in the section along the Spree River is home to several venues, including the **Berliner Ensemble**, founded in 1949 by Bertolt Brecht and Helene Weigel. The legendary **Deutsche Theater** became a European landmark during the 1920s due to the daring pro-

Theater des Westens (Theatre of the West).

ductions presented by director Max Reinhardt. Today, it mainly offers performances of the classics. Another historic room is the **Volksbühne**, or the People's Theatre, in Rosa-Luxemburg-Platz, a theatre built just before the First World War largely with donations from many poor people who always supported imaginative and innovative proposals in the period after German reunification. As for museums, there is something for everyone. A substantial number of them have been mentioned throughout the book. However, any list of essential or highly recommended museums must also include the **Jewish Museum** (an emotional tribute to the tragedy experienced by Berlin Jews during the years of the Nazi regime inaugurated in 2001; rooms like the Holocaust Tower, for example transmit the full horror of the period), the **Martin-Gropius-Bau** (a prestigious exhibition hall situated in an 1881 building by Martin Gropius) and next to it, the space known as the **Topography of Terror** (where the feared SS had their headquarters between 1933 and 1945). Others include the **Bauhaus Archive-Museum** (located in a building designed by the creator of the movement, Walter Gropius), the enormous and fascinating **German Technical Museum**, and the

Aerial view of Berlin Museum (Baroque palace) and the Jewish Museum.

Topography of Terror and, with the old Parliament of the Prussian States in the background.

The Hamburger Bahnhof.

Botanic Garden (inaugurated in 1910 and featuring more than 23,000 species in its 43 hectares; the collections of giant amphibious plants are particularly noteworthy). The four museums that make up the famous Dahlem complex, namely the **Museum of Indian Art**, the **Museum of Islamic Art**, the **Museum of Far Eastern Art**, and the **Ethnology Museum** (among the 500,000 objects are the rarities from five continents collected by the Prince Elector in the 17th century), the old **Hamburger Bahnhof** railway station (home to a small contemporary art museum including works by Andy Warhol, Roy Lichtenstein and Walter de Maria since 1996) and the **Communications Museum** (which spans the spectrum from postal communications to the latest data transmission innovations) round out our list.

German Technical Museum.

Botanic Garden: the Tropical Greenhouse.

FESTIVALS

Of the numerous events celebrated in Berlin, we have selected the three which draw the largest crowds. The first is the **Love Parade**, the huge electronic music festival celebrated in Tiergarten by thousands of young people in July. The Love Parade began in the 1980s as a party for techno fans and quickly became enormously popular, with 1,500,000 people attending in 1999. Interest later waned, to the point where the 2004 and 2005 Parades were never held but it made a comeback with renewed force in 2006. The second is the **Carnival of Cultures**, a large street celebration held in May in honour of the extraordinary mix of ethnicities living in the city. The third celebration is the **Christopher Street Day** gay pride parade, with colourful and musical floats travelling down an eight kilometre route between Ku'Damm and Tiergarten. The Christopher Street Day celebration is a reminder of the police assaults on homosexuals in Christopher Street in New York in June 1969 that signalled the birth of movements defending the rights of homosexuals.

Three images from the Christopher Street Day celebration.

POTSDAM

Potsdam, situated about 20 kilometres from Berlin, boasts some of the most beautiful palaces in Europe. That began to become apparent in the 17th century, when the princes of Brandenburg chose Potsdam as their residence. In 1701, the Prussian King and Queen noticed Potsdam and erected new mansions of unique beauty there. When the Second World War ended, the capital of the *land* (state) of Brandendurg became the setting for the meetings of the Allied Powers who would determine Germany's future. Also dubbed the "Versailles of the North", it is also a reference for cinema lovers. Fantastic movies such as "Faust" by Fritz Lang, and "The Blue Angel", with the unforgettable Marlene Dietrich as the main character, were filmed there. It goes without saying that the **Cinema Museum**, which is

Aerial view of the city of Potsdam. Behind the city is the Havel, the Grunewald woods and Berlin. In the box, the Old Market Square with the Church of Saint Nicholas and the Old Town Hall, and the Cinema Museum.

particularly informative on the history of the famous DEFA studios in the cinema city of Babelsberg, is a pilgrimage site for fans of the seventh art.

Declared a UNESCO World Heritage Site in 1990, the Sans-Souci palace and its gardens are Potsdam's most valued treasures. Friedrich II had the idea to construct this marvellous complex. He only wanted to have a modest residence where he could forget the tribulations and tensions he had to bear. It was named **Sans-Souci Palace**, French for "no worries", for that reason.

In 1745, the architect for the project, Hans Geog von Knobelsdorff, designed the small palace on some terraced vineyards. It occupies a total area of 290 hectares, including the gardens.

New buildings added to the complex over the years only increased its standing. The **China House** was erected between 1754 and 1757, the **Neptune's Grotto** between 1751 and 1757, the **Painting Gallery** between 1755 and 1764, and the **New**

89

The Historic Mill and the China House (overview and detail of the highest part).

Chambers built in 1747 were converted into a residence between 1771 and 1775.

At the end of the Seven Years' War (1756-1763), Prussia's strength and glory were reflected in the **New Palace**, built between 1763 and 1769. It became the main building in the Sans-Souci complex, with 200 luxuriously decorated rooms, 292 sculptures, 196 large angel figures, various laurel crowns carved in stone, and a majestic dome covering the palace. The **Communities** are found behind the palace. They were created between 1766 and 1769 for the servants.

When Friedrich Wilhelm IV, crowned in 1840, was Prince, the park in Sans-Souci was enlarged again. The **Charlottenhof Castle**, built between 1826 and 1829, the **Roman Baths** and the **Court Garden House**, both from 1829, and the **Greenhouse**, a project from 1828 not carried out until 1860, all date from this period.

In Luisenplatz, in the city of Potsdam, we can admire the **Brandenburg Gate**, the triumphal arch built in 1771 to commemorate the vic-

tory of the Seven Years' War. Nearby, towards the south, is the **Old Market**, the **Church of Saint Nicholas** and the **Old Town Hall**. The **Dutch District** extends between Bassinplatz and the neo-Gothic **Nauener Gate**, which dates from 1755. This complex of red-brick houses was once the home of the Dutch craftsmen contracted by Frederick the Great to work on the urban development of the city. The district, built between 1734 and 1742, was forgotten during the early years of the GDR. Shortly before the unification, the eastern authorities had undertaken an ambitious rehabilitation plan that was continued in the following years. Today, it is one of the most beautiful areas in Potsdam.

Dutch District.

The **Marble Palace** is situated by the banks of the Heiligen Lake. The brick and Silesian marble building was Friedrich Wilhelm II's favourite residence. Also in the north is the **Russian Colony**, some Russian-style houses dating from 1826 that were converted into the site of the Russian Orthodox church three years later, and the **Cecilienhof Castle.** The latter building is part of contemporary world history for hosting the July 1945 meetings between the heads of state and government of the victorious countries in the Second World War. Stalin, Truman and Churchill signed the agreement that would mark Germany's history in the years to come. The round table where these leaders signed their names is one of the objects that can be seen inside. It was built between 1913 and 1916 to look exactly like an English country house and has now been transformed into a hotel and restaurant.

Babelsberg Castle is found in the park of the same name, very close to the lake. It was built between 1835 and 1849 by Friedrich Wilhelm II, who modelled it on Windsor Castle. It was later expanded to accommodate a larger number of guests.

The Marble Palace, next to Heiligen Lake.

CONTENTS

EDITORIAL FISA
ESCUDO DE ORO, S.A.
www.eoro.com

S C H I K K U S
VERLAG & GROSSHANDEL
www.schikkus.de

I.S.B.N. 978-84-378-2869-5
Printed in Spain
Legal Dep. B. 47578-2008